CW01090734

# DISCIPLED TO CHRIST

# DISCIPLED TO CHRIST

As Seen in the Life of Simon Peter

STEPHEN KAUNG

Christian Fellowship Publishers, Inc.
New York

ISBN 0-935008-17-9

Available from the Publishers at:

11515 Allecingie Parkway
Richmond Virginia 23235
www.c-f-p.com

Printed in the United States of America

# PREFACE

THE CALL of discipleship comes to all believers in Christ. The word of the Lord to His own is, Come ye after Me. He intends to re-make us according to His image and to use us according to His purpose. Only in response to this call can we fulfill the destiny foreordained by God.

To help us understand this exceedingly important subject, the three chapters of this little volume illustrate —through the life of Simon Peter—the three principal aspects of Christian discipleship, namely: the call, the condition, and the consolation of discipleship. It is the person of the Lord Jesus to whom we are discipled—not to any system, organization, teaching or individual, but to one man and one man only, the Lord Jesus himself. Discipleship is not without its conditions, though the fulfilling of them lies in the pure grace of God. And although the hardship incurred in discipline is sometimes not pleasant, it is more than compensated for by the fellowship of the Master and the transformation which follows such fellowship.

May the Blessed Master encourage many into true discipleship.

# CONTENTS

## Editor's Note

A word should be appended regarding the sources for the material found in the following pages. First, the substance of the three Chapters making up this volume was originally a sequence of messages which the author delivered at Mt. Lake, Connecticut before a special young people's conference held during the New Year's weekend, January 1967. And second, as an added enrichment to the entire volume, the author kindly loaned to the editor his set of private preparatory notes containing many gold nuggets scattered throughout, a sizeable number of which never found their way into the messages subsequently spoken but are now included here.

Scripture quotations are from the
American Standard Version
of the Bible (1901),
unless otherwise indicated.

# CHAPTER ONE

# THE CALL OF DISCIPLESHIP

One of the two that heard John speak, and followed him, was Andrew, Simon Peter's brother. He findeth first his own brother Simon, and saith unto him, We have found the Messiah (which is, being interpreted, Christ). He brought him unto Jesus. Jesus looked upon him, and said, Thou art Simon the son of John: thou shalt be called Cephas (which is by interpretation, Peter). (John 1.40–42)

And walking by the sea of Galilee, he saw two brethren, Simon who is called Peter, and Andrew his brother, casting a net into the sea; for they were fishers. And he saith unto them, Come ye after me, and I will make you fishers of men. And they straightway left the nets, and followed him. And going on from thence he saw other two brethren, James the son of Zebedee, and John his brother, in the boat with Zebedee their father, mending their nets; and he called them. And they straightway left the boat and their father, and followed him. (Matt. 4.18–22)

Now it came to pass, while the multitude pressed upon him and heard the word of God, that he was standing by the lake of Gennesaret; and he saw two boats standing by the lake: but the fishermen had gone out of them, and were washing their nets. And he entered into one of the boats, which was Simon's, and asked him to put out a little from the land. And he sat down and taught the multitudes out of the boat. And when he had left speaking, he said unto Simon, Put out into the deep, and let down your nets for a draught. And Simon answered and said, Master, we toiled all night, and took nothing: but at thy word I will let down the nets. And when they had done this, they inclosed a great multitude of fishes; and their nets were breaking; and they beckoned unto their partners in the other boat, that they should come and help them. And they came, and filled both the boats, so that they began to sink. But Simon Peter, when he saw it, fell down at Jesus' knees, saying, Depart from me; for I am a sinful man, O Lord. For he was amazed, and all that were with him, at the draught of the fishes which they had taken; and so were also James and John, sons of Zebedee, who were partners with Simon. And Jesus said unto Simon, Fear not; from henceforth thou shalt catch men. And when they had brought their boats to land, they left all, and followed him. (Luke 5.1–11)

THE CALL of discipleship, someone has observed, is a very personal one, and because of that it has to be answered personally. But the call of discipleship is also a practical one, and therefore it has to be experienced in our life. Such a call is not a theory nor a doctrine but is something to which each one of us must give answer before the Lord and must experience, we hope, positively and not negatively. Now as a help to our understanding of just how personal and just how real experientially it is, I would like to demonstrate this subject of discipleship by briefly reviewing the life of one disciple of our Lord Jesus. And I can think of no better example than the life of Simon Peter.

Simon Peter was among the first of those who came to know the Lord, and most certainly he was one of the first called to be a disciple. Among the twelve apostles he was always the one listed first, and it was he who usually spoke for the others. Hence I think we may put it this way, that Simon Peter can be viewed as the first disciple of our Lord Jesus. And if he was indeed the first disciple of the Lord, then by virtue of this fact we can learn much from this man's life. In other words, all the principles involved in discipleship ought to be very easily discernible through a study of this one life.

TO BEGIN WITH, Simon was first brought to the Lord through his brother Andrew. Andrew had been introduced to Christ by John the Baptist. And Andrew, having found the Lord, next went to find his brother. Whereupon he simply told Simon Peter, "We have found the Messiah," and led him to Christ. Thus, in this very natural way, was this man Simon saved.

✳

WE DO NOT KNOW MUCH about Simon's past before he
first met the Lord. It would appear as though his prom-
inence and importance only came with his acquaintance
with the Lord Jesus. Two facts concerning Simon's
prior history, however, do stand out. We know first of
all that he was a man of Galilee, a native of the city of
Bethsaida (John 1.44). Also, that he was a fisherman.

We know that at that time the Jews elsewhere in Israel looked down upon the Galileans. In a very correct
sense the Galileans were Jews allright, but in another
sense those who lived in Galilee were viewed by those
Jews who lived in Jerusalem and Judea as being of
"Galilee of the nations" (Matt. 4.15 mg.)—for they
were a mixed multitude of impure, unorthodox, unrefined, not too well-cultured peoples. Nevertheless, it
should be observed that among the twelve disciples of
our Lord Jesus all of them, including Simon himself,
were Galileans, except probably Judas Iscariot who
may have been from Judea.

Simon, then, was a Galilean, a rough, unrefined
fisherman who, though his profession was lowly, had a
noble aspiration: he was looking for the coming of the
Jewish Messiah. Although outwardly he was rough, inwardly he was pious. Simon was naturally of an impul-
sive nature, outspoken, aggressive and quick in temper—
yet honest, sincere and unassuming. He was buried and
lost in the earth among the multitudes until Christ came
along and dug him up and transformed this rough stone
into, as we shall see, a beautiful precious jasper.

Yet this transformation can be true of all of us. Wherever we may have been born, and regardless of whatever nature and temperament we possess, no matter the profession we may be in or trained for, and however different we may be in our outward appearance and expression, the Lord is able to dig us up out of the crowd and commence to work in us till we become precious stones for the building of His house. We can therefore take courage in Simon Peter who, being of no importance to the world, was nevertheless taken and formed by the Lord into one of the pillars of the church at Jerusalem.

THE CONVERSION of Simon Peter was very simple. Most likely he had become a disciple of John the Baptist, since all those who were then looking for the Consolation of Israel (Luke 2.25) had been baptized by John. He had repented of his sins, had been baptized by the Baptist, and was currently looking forward to the Messiah who was to come—He who was to be the Sent One, the Anointed One of God, the One who would fulfill all God's promises. In other words, we find in this man Simon a ready heart, one who was prepared ahead of time by God's Spirit and no doubt by John the Baptist as well. Everything was therefore ready. The only thing left for him was to see the Messiah. And this came about throught the quiet witness of Simon's brother Andrew, whom we are definitely sure came to know Jesus as the Messiah through the testimony of John the Baptist. And thereafter Andrew went with haste to find his brother and confidently said to him, We have found the Messiah. With the result that Simon went, he saw, and he believed.

I BELIEVE SIMON had much confidence in his brother. From the record of his life we know that Simon was a man who was quick, outspoken, and not very careful. But his brother was just the opposite. Andrew was a very quiet man, and a quiet man is usually careful and quite observant. This latter trait is borne out in the incident of the feeding of the five thousand. You will remember that once when our Lord Jesus was in the wilderness there was nothing to eat, and it was Andrew who came and said, "There is a little boy here who has . . ." Think of it! Out of 5,000 people he noticed a small lad! That was Andrew's keen sense of observation. Hence I believe Simon, knowing his own weakness, had much confidence in his brother. He found in Andrew his need. He could trust his brother's discovery of the Messiah and thus be led to Christ. It is a good thing sometimes to recognize our own lack or weakness and to know how to be interdependent—especially with our brothers and sisters—because that brother or sister of ours may be able to provide the balance we need. So I feel that Simon, when his brother came and told him he had found the Messiah, had no doubt in his heart, but on the contrary must have thought within himself: "My brother Andrew must have found the *real* one." And so

Simon unhesitatingly went with him to see Jesus. Oh how blessed are the ready and the uncomplicated—those who know and acknowledge their own lack—for they shall quickly be filled.

✳

NOW THE BIBLE does not mention anything of Simon's reaction to the Lord. The Scriptures only tell us that he was led to Christ. Actually, I would have expected that when Simon, being by nature a very talkative person, had seen the Lord Jesus he would have spoken a great deal. Yet strangely enough, there is no record of his having said anything to the Lord—not so much as a word. He went and saw Jesus; and in the encounter he must have looked Him over very carefully; and the more he looked at Him the more he became convinced that this was the Messiah. With the result that Simon simply fell all over the Lord. He was so thrilled, so absorbed, so attracted by this Man that the one who all his life had been so talkative now fell silent—he had not a word to say. In the event, no word was necessary. It was a silent, quiet, reverent trust in the Messiah. The most vocal became speechless; he was too engrossed with what he saw.

And in gazing at Jesus with such wonder and adoration, the whole heart of Simon went out to the Lord in faith and trust. For at that critical moment a revelation came to him; the Father revealed the Son to Simon Peter. We know this to be true because of what the Lord said to Peter about Simon's declaration of faith which he had uttered in a full public confession of Christ years later at a time when Jesus was being rejected by His own people. In that instance the Lord had said to Peter that his understanding of Him as the Christ did not have its source in flesh and blood but had been revealed to him by the Father in heaven (Matt. 16.17). And surely this revelation had not just then come to Peter; but on the contrary this first full public confession of Christ referred back to what Peter had experienced at the time of his very first encounter with the Lord when his brother Andrew had led him to the Messiah. And as Simon now approached the Messiah in simplicity and readiness of heart he received a revelation concerning the Lord.

Yet this will always be the case, because the will of God is hidden from the wise and clever but is revealed to the babes (Luke 10.21). Revelation is given to the simple, to those who live by the heart and not by the head. And as soon as Simon Peter received such revelation, he responded in quietness and sincerity of faith.

Very simple, was it not? Yet is that not the way we too must come to know the Lord? If you have a prepared heart and are looking for the Savior of mankind, and someone whom you can trust introduces this Savior to you, then just come to Him, look Him over, and you too, I believe, will be convinced, convicted and converted in the same way.

WE NEED TO NOTE that Andrew led Simon to *Jesus*. Not to a system of thought, not to a moral code of behavior, nor to a religious institution, but to Jesus Christ. Christ is the Savior. He is the Salvation for the lost. And if only we meet up with Christ and see Him, we shall be saved. For it is the person of Christ that attracts, and it is His work that saves. Have we met Him? This will solve all our problems and answer all our questions.

One sight of Jesus showed Simon that He truly was the Christ. "Blessed are the pure in heart: for they shall see God" (Matt. 5.8). One sight of Jesus is enough to convince us of the truthfulness of His Messiahship. But we do not see because we are not pure in heart—because we do not want Him. Too often our own natural ability and abundance form a stubborn line of resistance to our ever coming to know the Lord. Let me therefore ask: Have you come to know the Lord? Have you believed in His redemptive work? Have you trusted in His finished work on the cross? A simple trust out of an honest heart is all you need to bring to yourself all the value and merits of His perfect redemption. But if you do not come to the Lord Jesus with such a heart you will find it is difficult to believe in Him and your way to Him may be a very long, winding and even dangerous path. You may go the way of Saul of Tarsus, who being a most complex person, had to travel along a most circuitous and dangerous route before he was met by the Lord. Saul had to be struck blind to the ground before he would cry out to the Savior. But oh how much better if you can come to Him in simplicity and sincerity and be led by your heart and not misled by your mind. If only you will come to Him and look at Him, that will solve your problem. You will be saved. It is as easy and as natural as that. And I would hope that our coming to the Lord can be just as much this way as Simon Peter's once was.

\*

WE HAVE SEEN that Simon looked carefully at the Lord—sizing Him up from the head to the feet; and the more he gazed at Him the more he fell before Him. But we must observe from the record that the Lord did the same thing. When Simon was led to Christ, the Bible tells us that the Lord Jesus "looked upon him, and said, Thou art Simon, the son of John: thou shalt be called Cephas (which is by interpretation, Peter)" (John 1.42). It tells us that the Lord "looked upon" Simon Peter. Interestingly enough, this word means a viewing carefully. Jesus, in other words, *thoroughly* gazed at Simon.

Oh, the look of our Lord! That penetrating eye! He looked into the very heart and being of Simon with *spiritual insight*, and as our Lord gazed carefully at him He saw what the Spirit of God was doing at that very moment in his life: "Thou art Simon, but thou shalt be called Cephas—Peter." He thus was witness to the fact that the Spirit of God, in response to this man's childlike faith in Christ, had done the work of regeneration in Simon. It was done in Simon's spirit by the Holy Spirit, but the Lord as He spoke perceived it on the basis of what He saw in His own spirit.

But Jesus also looked into Simon Peter with *prophetic sight*. As He intently gazed at Simon He saw that in this man God had not only done something already but was also going to do an even greater thing in the future. "Thou art Simon the son of John," the Lord had said—as though meaning to say to Simon, This is the natural man, this is what you in yourself are, born as you are of your father John. But, the Lord went on, "Thou shalt be called Cephas"—Peter; that is to say, you shall be a new man, completely transformed into a new creation because born anew of the Spirit of God. Who was Simon anyway but the son of John—that which is made of dust, that which is earthy and common? And will he not be buried along with the rest of the world— unnoticed, a fisherman of no importance and nothing in himself? But now you shall be called by a new name: Peter, which means *a stone*.

A new element had today entered this Simon. Instead of remaining loose clay he has become a stone. A different kind of life has come into his spirit, and with that life a new nature and a new potential. He has become a stone. And we now know that this "living" stone is one day to become one of the twelve foundations of the city of New Jerusalem, and if in the mind of God he is listed as the first of the twelve apostles (Rev. 21.14) then he as the first stone of the twelve foundations is to be a jasper (Rev. 21.19). Can we see the progression here? From clay he becomes a stone, and this stone shall finally turn out to be a jasper. What is jasper? From Revelation 4 we learn that John saw the glory of the Lord God as though it were like a jasper. Think of it! Jasper—like unto the glory of the Lord himself!

NONE OF US KNOWS what is the potential and the possibility. None of us can foresee what God in fact can do with one in whom He has deposited His own life. Let us not boast of that which is natural in ourselves; it is nothing. It will fade away sooner or later, because its very nature is fleeting. But if within us we receive the life of Christ, no one can say what will be our future because there is such potential there. God can do great things if only we have His Son in us. In other words, the greatness is not in us; the greatness lies in His Son. And what a future can be ours as we believe in the Lord Jesus.

Hence we who are but clay, let us thank God that as we come to Christ we become as He is in life. Simon was nothing in himself, it was Christ alone who made him everything. Yet how true this is of everyone of us! He is that Living Stone from whom we too become those living stones that have been hewn out of the same mountainous rock. Long afterwards Simon Peter well understood this himself, for he wrote: "Unto whom coming, a living stone, rejected indeed of men, but with God elect, precious, ye also, as living stones, are built up a spiritual house, to be a holy priesthood, to offer up spiritual sacrifices, acceptable to God through Jesus Christ" (1 Peter 2.4–5).

It should be observed, however, that the Lord did not tell him here what would be the use to which this stone would be put. He reserved telling, until a later time, the purpose for working such a change in his life. Later on, as recorded in Matthew 16, we find that a further revelation is given him; namely, that this stone is going to become a part of the superstructure that is to be built upon the Rock, Christ Jesus, which not even the gates of hell will be able to prevail against. In other words, Simon Peter was to become one of the building materials comprising the church of God.

HERE, THEN, is the first incident in Peter's relationship to the Lord Jesus: how he came to know Christ and how, because of his trusting in Him, he became a stone. This is the point from which all of us must start. For without life the call of discipleship is impossible. God cannot call someone to be the Lord's disciple without there being any divine life. If we want to be His disciples we have to receive His life first. It is not essentially an outward imitation, it is first and foremost an inward transformation. And hence this is the reason why at the outset of our consideration of discipleship we must begin with the *conversion* of Simon Peter. And once this has taken place in Simon through the infusion of divine life, there is the possibility of discipleship.

LET US NEXT SHIFT to the second incident, and for this we need some background. John the Baptist, you will recall, was taken prisoner, and when the Lord Jesus heard of this He went to Galilee. He knew that from this moment onward He would have to bear the testimony of God alone since John was now removed from the scene. But Jesus felt He should gather around himself some disciples who could follow Him, be trained for the work the Father had asked Him to do, and who could then continue His task after His departure.

We therefore find from the record in Matthew 4 that one day shortly afterwards the Lord Jesus was walking by the Sea of Galilee; and while doing so He beheld two fishermen casting their nets into the water. One of them was Simon Peter and the other was his brother Andrew. So the Lord walked by and called to them, saying: "Come after Me, and I will make you fishers of men"— and immediately they left the nets and followed Him. The Lord could call them to follow Him because they had already accepted Him as Messiah and Savior. It was thus a call to discipleship. Now we do not know how long a period had passed between the time of Simon Peter's conversion and this call to discipleship. Most likely it was several months, perhaps even half a year; nevertheless, the Lord Jesus went along the seashore, saw him, and called him.

Yet what *was* the call? We need to read again this passage before us. The call was, "Come after Me and I will make you fishers of men." The emphasis is plainly laid on the "follow after me"—whereas the "fishers of men" will be the outcome. Ministry is always the result of discipleship. Let us carefully note that this is not primarily a call to service but is basically a call to discipleship. Yes, obviously, discipleship *is unto service;* but we must realize that the order of the call is first "Come after Me" and only secondarily is it "I will make you fishers of men." We must learn first and then we have something to give.

Hence we must be very sure not to reverse the order.

Too often in Christian lives is this the case, however. How people today lay so much stress on service, forgetting that only the disciple can truly serve. Too often, following our conversion experience, the first thought which in our zeal for the Lord takes shape in our thinking is, Now that I am saved, what can I *do* for the Lord? Is this not frequently how we view the matter? Of course, God knows our heart. And He appreciates it. Yet sooner or later we will learn that this is not the right order.

I WELL REMEMBER many years ago, when I was just in my teens, I was one day attending a summer conference. It was at this time that I was searching and seriously looking for salvation, for I was deeply burdened with my sins. And on this particular day of the conference I heard the gospel preached, and by the grace of God I came to the Lord in a very simple way and found all my burdens lifted. How happy I was—I was so grateful to the Lord. And so it happened that on the last day of this conference, and as was the traditional way in evangelical Christianity, there was a call for consecration, that is to say, a call to be a missionary was given. Oh, I can still recall the joy which was mine those many years ago when I was just saved. How much I was in love with the Lord! How He loved me and saved me! I just naturally wanted to give my life to Him, I wanted to serve Him. So that when the preacher gave his call for consecration to missionary service I was so eager to comply.

The preacher then said, "If there is any of you here who would like to serve the Lord you can come up to the platform and can choose your place. You just come on up here and point your finger at the place you wish to go to and serve the Lord" (and at this he turned and pointed towards a large map of China which was hanging behind him on the wall). When I heard this appeal I said to myself, Well, if I want to serve the Lord I want to serve Him in the farthest and most difficult place there is. And with that, I went up to the platform and pointed my finger unhesitatingly at Mongolia and declared that that was where I wanted to go!

Mercifully the Lord knew my ignorance. Moreover, I believe the Lord appreciates such naive ignorance. Nevertheless, we cannot overlook the fact that this is our natural concept. We quite naturally feel that the first thing in our life as a Christian is to do something for the Lord. Yes, we *must* do something for Him; the Lord, even expects this of us—eventually. But are we ready for that? Are we qualified for it?

Indeed I tried to make myself ready for it, because from that day onward it had become a serious matter for me. I began to look for books on Mongolia. I read volume after volume on that area of China and had set my mind fixedly on learning how to speak the Mongolian dialect. Furthermore, I prayed each day for a whole year —every morning praying, "Lord, I am going to Mongolia; just You get me ready for it." And after I had graduated from high school I decided that the only way for me to learn to preach the gospel was to go for training to a Bible school. Whereupon I picked out a school and said to my parents that there was where I wanted to go and prepare myself. But how disappointed I was when my father said no.

How I would have us all understand this one thing, that the call to discipleship must *precede* the call to service. For we shall see that discipleship is the basis for usefulness and effectiveness in our lives. As children of God we receive everything from Him for our nourishment and growth. And as disciples of Christ we are still receiving from the Master, although it is a receiving not merely for our own good but also for being made into fit vessels for the Master's use. So let us remember that the right order is first a disciple and then a minister.

✳

IN THE OLD DAYS a disciple was different from a student. Today we think of them as being the same: that is to say, a person will pay some money and he then attends a college, a professional school, a technical institute, or whatever it may be, where the teacher or instructor is paid a salary out of the person's money and is going to instruct and teach him all he knows about the skill, the trade, the learning, or profession concerned. And there the person sits, listening and taking in and absorbing all of it until finally he exhausts the teacher's knowledge of his subject or skill. With the result that, being as well learned and skillful as his teacher, he then graduates and goes out and does the very thing his instructor did: having obtained a degree, he himself becomes a master!

In this we can see that there is no intimate life relationship between the professor and his student. It is but a meeting of mind with mind, not a life with life. The whole process is almost totally mental in scope. And after the four or so years are completed, a person goes away with his own mind filled with his professor's mind, but the person's life still remains his own. Now that is the modern way of being a disciple and learning.

According to the Bible, however, this thing of being a disciple is seen in an entirely different light. We may use a quite common word to describe it, the word *apprentice*. And this term conjures up the relationship which exists between an apprentice in a trade and his master. But what exactly does this mean? Well, let us say that your father arranges to have you placed in apprenticeship to a master in some trade or craft; and if this master is willing to accept you as his apprentice it is considered to be a privilege and an honor to you. Yes, you will have to pay your master something, but that is not thought of as salary. Not at all. You instead pay him out of a sense of honoring your master because he is willing to take you. Sometimes, though, a master is not willing to take a given student or apprentice. He may feel there is no potential in you, that it would be just a waste of time to take you to himself. In other words, it is a matter of qualification and not the ability to pay; what he considers is whether you can be a successful apprentice or not, and this determines the matter. It is your privilege and honor to be accepted as an apprentice. Not his honor, your honor.

Then too, in the olden days, when anyone became an

apprentice he would not live at home. At that time, if you were given an apprenticeship you would leave your own home, cut off all relationships, and move to your master's dwelling and live with him. You would stay with him day and night, and perhaps during the first year he would not teach you a thing; he would only ask you to help with his household jobs. For example, you might have to hold his baby, you might be required to sweep the floor, or some other such task. But, you might ask, what have these chores to do with apprenticeship? I came to learn a skill! But no, in older times, you had to begin from the *very* beginning. A whole year might pass by without the master teaching you anything; you are merely doing these menial jobs as a servant to a master.

Gradually, though, the master commences to tell you this or to show you that, or to correct you in the other thing. And after a few years of this—when the term of your apprenticeship has terminated—you discover you have learned not only the skill or craft of your master but more so the mannerism of your master, the philosophy of life of your master; and not only so, but very often the way you now walk and the way you now talk has become very much like your master; it is a reproduction of the master himself. The life as well as the skill of the master is being reproduced in his apprentice. A disciple is therefore not someone putting something on, he in reality is being transformed into another man.

✳

INTERESTINGLY ENOUGH, the Lord's call to become a

disciple came to those who were busy. It would seem as if He has no need of the idle, the lazy, or indifferent. It is instructive to note that Jesus called Peter when the latter was fishing. He called Levi at the customs house. And He called Saul while he was busily engaged in persecuting the believers. Our Lord *chooses* as His disciples those who have potential and can be trained. Yet let us not forget this fact that *all* of God's children are *called* to be His disciples. Unfortunately, though, not all hear the call. Let us therefore see that it is a great honor to hear the Lord's call for discipleship; and having heard, we ought to rise up and follow Him—recognizing what a privilege is ours to be permitted to do so.

NOW THE CALL to discipleship is actually a very easily understood one. The Lord says, Come after Me, Follow Me. That is all. He does not say follow this or follow that; come after this or come after that. The Lord merely says, Come after Me—*Me!* Just as it was in your conversion, it is the person of the Lord Jesus to whom you are discipled—not to any system, not to any organization, not to any teachings, not to anybody but to one man and one man only, and that is the Lord Jesus. "Come after Me" is the call. You are not called to believe, or follow, or to comply with some rules and regulations. Not so. You are summoned to be disciples of a living person: Christ himself. And because He is living and not something fixed or static, you never know what will happen. You just cannot figure it out. In short, you are to *follow* Him.

And so it was that when the Lord said, Come after Me and I will make you fishers of men, Peter left his net and followed Him. So easy! So uncomplicated! The Lord did not explain to Peter why he must follow Him, the Lord did not even tell him at that time what would be the cost. Nor did He explain to him the meaning of following Him—for example, Christ never said a word such as, Peter, leave your net and follow Me. Not even that. If you can bring your net and pursue after Christ, all right. But Peter knows he cannot. No, the Lord merely said to follow Him. And Peter left his net and went after Him. Now why?

Peter of course knew the Lord. He was not a stranger to Peter. By revelation he had seen Jesus as the Christ, the Son of the living God, in whom was his hope and the hope of Israel. He had perfect trust in the Lord. And thus, the only reason why Peter, with no hesitation, could leave everything and follow the Lord was simply because he was attracted by that Person who was calling him.

If in this experience of discipleship you look at yourself or look around or try to figure out (now there *is* a place for this in discipleship, and I will come to that later), you will surely hesitate: Can the cost be too great? Can the Master be too harsh? This is a *hard* thing—how then can I ever answer Him? Yes, it is quite true, that if your eyes are upon yourself or upon the things around you it is very difficult to answer the call. But if you are like Peter, that is, if you have seen the Lord and have heard Him, if you are attracted by the glory of that Person, then there is no argument, no calculation, and no reservation. The response will be both natural and easy. When He calls, you go. And that was the way it was with Simon Peter.

IN THIS MATTER of discipleship there *are* two sides: on the one side it does demand careful consideration, but on the other side there ought to be neither hesitation nor consideration of any kind, for it is *beyond* all that. And why? Because you are attracted by this Person. If discipleship is based upon anything else than the person of our Lord Jesus, then you must indeed consider, there is most certainly room for hesitation. But if discipleship is based upon the Master himself, where ever is there room for consideration? Let us see that if you consider, you disgrace your Master—He who so loved us and gave himself for us, He who is the Lord of the universe, He who is your Redeemer, your King, your life, hope, and everything. So that when One such as *this* calls, what *can* you do but go, and without the slightest reservation quickly rise up and follow Him.

Hence my prayer is that Christ will reveal himself to us. Let us not be drowned in many thoughts: How much I must leave behind, must forsake or must give up— How my life will be dull and miserable without these things—What sacrifices I will have to make—What must become of me afterwards. Permit me to say that if you are like this, you have *not* seen the Lord. But if you *have*

seen the Lord, then these things most surely fade away.
For when the Master calls, you just go because you are
following *Him*. And such is the call of discipleship. Peter left all and followed Jesus. And he found that the
forsaking was more than compensated for by the companionship of his Lord.

WE NEXT MOVE ON to the third incident. It is recorded in
Luke chapter 5. Several months had probably gone by
and during these months Simon Peter had been following Jesus. We know that during the first stage of the
Lord's ministry he accompanied Him both in Judea and
in Galilee. Hence for several months Peter witnessed
many things the Lord had done and said. Even so, we
find that somehow (though we do not know how or why
it came about) he was once again fishing. And once
more the Lord came back for him.

We do not know whether in the early stages the understanding between Jesus and His disciples was un-
clear or what. Was it because in the beginning of His
ministry the Lord did not require His disciples to be always with Him? Or was it because Peter did not know
the full meaning of discipleship, thinking he could serve
two masters at the same time? We cannot be sure. Yet
we do notice this, that when the call of discipleship came
initially to Simon Peter he did respond quickly and
thoroughly at that moment. But it took some little time
before the full meaning of the call took hold of his life.
For we know from the biblical account that Peter both

followed the Lord and did not follow the Lord: he was
an on-and-off disciple. There was still the pull towards
other centers in his life. So that it took another crisis to
stabilize Simon Peter and make him permanent in his
discipleship—a crisis such as the one in his life now before us. For we shall discover that the incident of the miraculous catch of fish that eventful morning stirred Peter
to the very center of his heart.

WHAT DID HAPPEN that morning when the Lord Jesus
found him once again by the shore of the Sea of Galilee?
Well, we find that Peter and his companions had fished
the whole night through and could not catch a thing. It
had been a very disappointing experience—a long, cold,
windy night with nothing to show for their efforts. And
here he was with his brother and partners, all of them
washing their nets on the morning after. And it was during this particular morning that Jesus came by and a
great multitude gathered to hear Him. So much so that
the Lord told Peter to move his boat out a little to avoid
His being crowded; and then Jesus spoke to the crowds
from the safety of the boat.

But after He had spoken (and as though not wishing
to use the boat free of charge), the Lord commanded Peter, "Go to the deep, throw your nets, and have a haul."
Simon must have looked at Jesus in utter amazement.
Can you not almost see the expression on his face, as if
to say: "You are not a fisherman, and yet You tell me

*this?* Don't You know that I am an *expert?*" Nevertheless, Peter in his reply explained: "Master, we have fished all night and have gotten nothing." By this statement he perhaps expected the Lord to take back His word. He hoped, perhaps, for the Lord to retract by saying: "I'm sorry; since an expert has explained his expert opinion, I withdraw My idea entirely." Yet Jesus did not take back His word. So that Simon Peter, out of respect for Him as his Master, continued by saying that at His word he would do as the Lord had commanded.

We need to note, however, that in His command the Lord used a plural number, "nets" (v.4). In other words, *both* boats were to go out and *both* nets were to be cast—not only Peter and Andrew's but also the boat and net belonging to James and John. But Peter only used one boat and net (v.5,6 Darby); and consequently his own net was nearly broken. What this tells us of Peter is that he believed the Lord in only a half-hearted way. After all, if there was anything he really knew as an expert, it was fishing. And if he—as an expert—had fished all night and gotten nothing, how then could a carpenter, who knew nothing about fish, order him to cast his net into the deep for a haul? He could only half-heartedly respond. "All right, we'll do it," Peter had said. But only he and his brother Andrew would do it, leaving James and John his partners behind because he thought it was a hopeless task.

Yet we know what happened. When Simon Peter threw the net into the water it came up full of fishes and was nearly broken, and he even had to call his partners on shore to come and help pull up the gigantic haul.

And it was at this dramatic moment that something quite unusual happened to Peter.

THE GOSPEL OF LUKE records it this way: Simon Peter, seeing it, fell at Jesus' knees saying, "Depart from me; for I am a sinful man, O Lord" (5.8). A glimpse of the Master as Lord now made Peter feel so ashamed of his sinful heart that he prostrated himself at the feet of Jesus and asked the Lord to leave him. He keenly sensed, at one incredible stroke, the moral distance between himself and the Lord.

Yet did not Peter know the Lord? He did. He knew Him as the Christ, the Son of the living God. He had witnessed many things done by Him, had heard many words spoken by Him. Peter quite well knew the Lord, and yet in another sense he did not know Him. Yes, he called Jesus his Master, the One who was over him. Even so, when this miracle occurred before him, Peter's eyes were opened as they had never been opened before. He for the first time saw that this Christ—this Jesus—this carpenter from Nazareth—was none other than the Lord of the universe. He had control over everything, even over the fishes of the sea! This Man was indeed the Master, and Peter now realized how he had treated Him. For it could be said that during this period Simon had been a man who for a while had gone along with the Lord as a disciple, but having other interests he had gone back and fished some more. When he had initially responded to the Lord in such great boldness Peter could not have known what discipleship actually involved, nor did he genuinely know himself in relationship to it. But during the ensuing months of intermittent companionship with the Lord, Simon undoubtedly commenced for the first time in his life to perceive—even if vaguely— something of himself as he really was.

We can only surmise a little as to what must have gone through this disciple's heart during that period. Yet most likely the Master must have been growing bigger and bigger in Peter's eyes while by comparison he himself was growing less and less. He might even have begun to wonder if the Master had made a good choice in him; for although he called the Lord his Master and wanted to serve Him and be His disciple, it no doubt began to dawn upon him that, as a matter of fact Jesus was *not* the center of his life, that he still had his own interests, he still wanted his own way. In short, he had become a man who found himself continually halting between two opinions. Consequently, Peter could no longer feel so sure of himself: On the one hand he wished he could throw himself in completely, on the other hand he wanted to quit. On the one hand he could not tear himself away from the Lord—He had attracted him so much, but on the other hand he could not go all out for the Lord because there were other things constantly pulling him back. Here, then, was a man of double-mindedness, of double love, double interest, double loyalty. Oh what spiritual conflict raged within this soul! Obviously he was a man trying to serve two masters instead of one, yet because of this he was a disciple of none. To his sorrow he had learned nothing. It had been a waste of time.

Is this not true in your own experience? You too may have responded to the Lord with unhesitating boldness and declared: "Yes, Lord, I will follow You." But what happened after you started to follow Him as your Master? You gradually became aware that there was the pull towards other centers in your life. You commenced to observe the unpleasant fact that in your heart there was another master; and how reluctant you were, you discovered, to give up that mastership. And like Peter, your walk too became an off-and-on following of the Lord. What you needed was a crisis to stir you to the depths of your being, an experience that, like Peter's, would shatter your previous conduct and your earlier conception of things.

Now when Simon recognized that the Lord knew more about fishing than Simon the expert fisherman knew, that this Person is more, even, than an expert— He being the One who has absolute knowledge and control over all things—then he realized that Christ must be the Lord of all in his own life or else He is not Lord in his life at all. With lightning speed, and by means of this extraordinary event, the true meaning of discipleship finally broke in upon this wavering disciple. At long last he saw how impossible it was for him to serve two masters. Either Christ must be my *only* Master and Lord,

Peter now acknowledged, or else I have to ask Him to depart from me, for I am not worthy.

How truly ironic! Originally it was Jesus who had called him to be His disciple, but now it was a case of Peter having to decide whether he *could be* his Master's disciple or not.

Just here we must try to feel as Peter felt that day. He had said to the Lord, "Depart from me, for I am a sinful man." Yet did he really want the Lord to depart from him? If he did, why did he simply not walk away himself from the Lord? He certainly was free to do so. Yet Peter found he could not depart from the Master. Jesus in His moral glory had greatly attracted him, so much so that what in reality he begged of his Master was this: "Lord, I cannot leave You—I am bound to You; yet I am unworthy. You called me to be Your disciple, but I am unfit to be Your disciple. The past few months *prove* that I am not, that I'm not true to You. I cannot overcome myself. I want to be my own master too much, I want to have my own way; so that I do not know what to do with myself. And I still don't know. I dare not cheat You and try to fool You by saying I am willing to go all the way with You—when I cannot. For I find that there are other ties and other attractions which pull me back. Lord, do You really want me to be Your disciple—such a man as I? Maybe You have chosen the wrong person. I am really unfit. O Lord, do let me go, please. Do not spoil Your work and Your purpose. *I* cannot leave, for I am drawn to You, I am bound to You, I am even called by You; but Lord, You can release me if You feel like doing so."

Such must have been the feeling of this man when he said, "Depart from me, depart from me!" Peter had such a low opinion of himself that he asked the Lord to depart from him a sinful man. Yet, as was asked before, *did* he want the Lord to leave him? Certainly not. "Oh, if only You will *not* depart!" Peter must have thought. "Yet dare I ask You not to leave, knowing I am a sinful man?" Such a statement, it should be clearly understood, was not uttered in the sense that he was unregenerated but in the sense that he was a double-minded person, a half-hearted man, a man who held two allegiances. Outwardly he was following the Lord, inwardly he was not. A pretense and a failure in utterness: *that* is his sin. "I am a sinful man," confessed Peter, "and I can only ask for You to depart from me because that is what I deserve. I am not worthy."

If we can enter into the depths of Peter's feelings we can perhaps understand the issue. He could not leave the Lord, and so in his humility he now asked the Lord to leave him, to cast him away as unworthy and unfit to be His disciple. Peter could no longer trust himself, he was unsure of his perseverance; in fact, he was almost sure he would fail.

UNLESS THE LORD has led you to this point that Peter experienced, I am afraid your discipleship may not be firm and sealed. Are you presently in such a condition? You know that the Lord has called you to be His disciple, which is to say, He has called you to be with Him, to follow Him and to learn of Him that you may be like Him. But after you have quickly responded you begin to know the wickedness of your heart; you discover you are reluctant to give up your mastership over yourself; you want to be your own master and are thus torn between two loyalties. And perhaps one day Christ reveals to you concerning His glory that He is the *Lord* of all. Oh! He is your Lord. He demands that you give Him your whole allegiance, that you surrender yourself completely to Him, that you put yourself in His hands and let Him mold and shape you as He would like to because He is your Master. On the one hand you want to, on the other hand you cannot do so. Thus do you waver between these two things, so much so that perhaps this becomes *your* prayer: "Depart from me, O Lord, for I am not worthy." Yet, like Peter, you do not want Him to go away from you. You want Him to have you.

Let me put it to you once again, Have you come to this point? If you have, then hear carefully what the Lord replied to Peter. Said Jesus: "*Fear not*; from henceforth thou shalt catch men" (Luke 5.10).

LET US SEE that to be the Lord's disciple it cannot be based upon your own strength, it has to come from Him. He is the One who calls and He is the One who will work it out. It does not depend upon yourself. Do not think because you have an iron will you can be His disciple; do not assume because you have natural love you can be His disciple; do not think because you understand you can therefore be His disciple. If you try to be a follower by relying upon yourself you will completely fail. If you try to be absolute with the Lord in and of yourself, let me tell you that you cannot. It is impossible. With man this is utterly impossible. Nevertheless, you need not be afraid. The Lord knows you. The Lord does not expect you to be His disciple on your own basis. For hear again the gracious words of the Lord: "Fear not, I am with you; I will do it; you are but clay in My hand."

I am reminded of the story in the life of Jeremiah. We are told in chapter 18 that the prophet went down to a potter's house and saw a man turning a mound of clay on his wheel. And as he turned the wheel and tried to form a vessel, the latter became marred in the potter's hands. That is a picture of Simon Peter in the hands of the master Potter: for there was resistance, there were foreign particles, Peter as a vessel was marred and broken before it was even made. But as in the case of the potter in Jeremiah's day, the master Potter did not throw this human clay away. He took up the same material and began again to form it into a new vessel as seemed good to the Potter to make.

Oh the skill of the Master! It does not depend upon you and me, it depends upon the hand of the Master. In ourselves we are broken, we are marred, we cannot be a good vessel—broken already before it is made, before it is fit for use. Nevertheless, the Lord says, "Fear not; I will mold you, I will make a new vessel out of you." How comforting that word must have been to Simon. "Do not be afraid, Peter; it is not how much you are that matters, it is I who will make you a fisher of men. If it should depend on you, you will fail as you yourself feel. But if it depends on Me, you will catch men for the kingdom of God just as effortlessly as you caught these fishes today. So put yourself, just as you are, in My hands, and I will make a new vessel out of you."

The skill of the Master is shown in transforming the dullest and the most worthless into the wisest and the worthiest. All which is needed of the disciple is a full committal and willingness to learn. And so we see that Peter left everything and followed the Lord. And by such action this discipleship was sealed at last, and from that day onward we find Peter in the school of Christ— full time, totally committed, and following the Master.

*O Lord, show Yourself to us, show us Your glory. Make us to see You and hear You that we may respond to You as we ought. Reveal Yourself to us in all Your beauty, greatness and loveliness that we may be completely abandoned to You. So fill our hearts with Your love, Lord, that we may be constrained to rise up and follow You.*

*We do desire that Your image shall be seen through us as Your disciples. Yet Lord, evermore tell us that it does not depend upon ourselves to be a good disciple, but that it depnds upon You. May we learn to entrust ourselves into Your hands and let You mold and shape us to be a new vessel for Your glory. We ask that as You do call us, let none of us escape; even so, we cannot escape, for You have attracted us.*

*Lord, You know our hearts. Search us. Do not let this day pass by without something very real being done by Your Spirit in each one of us. To those who have not heard Your call, make us hear; to those who are hesitating, make us see You in all Your glory; to those who are afraid and feel unworthy—oh, overcome us by Your worthiness and by Your strength and obtain in us disciples for Yourself.*

*O Lord, we wait upon You, we trust You. We praise You and worship You, our worthy Lord, our worthy Master. In Your precious Name we pray. Amen.*

# CHAPTER TWO

# THE CONDITION OF DISCIPLESHIP

Peter began to say unto him, Lo, we have left all, and have followed thee. Jesus said, Verily I say unto you, There is no man that hath left house, or brethren, or sisters, or mother, or father, or children, or lands, for my sake, and for the gospel's sake, but he shall receive a hundredfold now in this time, houses, and brethren, sisters, and mothers, and children, and lands, with persecutions; and in the world to come eternal life. But many that are first shall be last; and the last first. (Mark 10.28–31)

Jesus said therefore unto the twelve, Would ye also go away? Simon Peter answered him, Lord, to whom shall we go? thou hast the words of eternal life. And we have believed and know that thou art the Holy One of God. Jesus answered them, Did not I choose you the twelve ... (John 6.67–71).

But Peter answered and said unto him, If all shall be offended in thee, I will never be offended. Jesus said unto him, Verily I say unto thee, that this night, before the cock crow, thou shalt deny me thrice. Peter saith unto him, Even if I must die with thee, yet will I not deny thee. Likewise also said all the disciples. (Matthew 26.33–35)

And the Lord turned, and looked upon Peter. And Peter remembered the word of the Lord, how that he said unto him, Before the cock crow this day thou shalt deny me thrice. And he went out, and wept bitterly. (Luke 22.61–62)

LAST TIME, we mentioned this subject of the call to discipleship and we saw how Simon Peter responded to that call. At first he responded swiftly and without hesitation, but we learned that later on he began to discover himself in relation to discipleship and it required a fresh vision of the Lord to strengthen him and to reinstate him in discipleship. And from that day onward for about three years Peter was apprenticed to the great Master, our Lord Jesus, and followed Him all the time. He was no longer a part-time disciple, nor an off-and-on disciple. From that moment forward he became a full-time follower of the Lord Jesus.

THIS DOES NOT MEAN, however, that after the Lord was taken away Peter was graduated from the school of discipleship. Nor does it mean that after Jesus had ascended to heaven Peter himself became a master. In one sense, yes, if we faithfully follow the Lord there *will* come a time when we shall become something akin to a little master under the great Master; but in another sense we never become masters; that is, we never come to that independence of will and action. Discipleship is therefore a lifetime occupation (until we are completed in Christ at His return), although we do move from apprenticeship into active duty to be used by the Lord to continue in the task He has begun. But even then, we never cease to be a disciple. In those three years of following Jesus, Peter learned much and yet he was never graduated; for after the ascension of the Lord, the promised Holy Spirit was poured out upon men and Peter thereafter was brought under *His* discipline and training. In short, he was a disciple for life.

Let it be clearly understood that when you answer the call of our Lord you are merely *beginning* in the way of discipleship. Do not think because you have responded to Christ you are therefore perfect, that you have everything, that you are a disciple full-fledged, mature, complete. Not so. When you respond to the call of discipleship it is only a starting point. From that day hence you will be under the discipline and the training of the Lord through His Holy Spirit, and He is going to transform you, mold you, and shape you until the Master shall be seen in you. There will never be a day in which you cease to learn. The more you learn of Him the more you have yet to learn because He is such a great Master. This I want to make clear at the outset.

✳

THE FOCUS of our consideration now turns to the very

important subject of the various conditions or pre-
requisites which must be present in our Christian discipleship. And we will discover that there are at least
three basic conditions which must be true in our experience if we expect to be good followers of our Lord Jesus.
And to demonstrate this we will look into a number of
different incidents from the life of Simon Peter which
candidly reveal his inner condition as a disciple of
Christ. Such incidents which we present here are in no
particular chronological order.

THE FIRST CONDITION of discipleship which should be
mentioned is that of *forsaking*. We must forsake all in
order to follow Him, because the Lord cannot do anything with us if the many old things of our lives still
bind us. The old habits, the old ties, the old creation— all
must be abandoned before He can do something new in
us. In the case of His disciples the Lord has no intention
of merely reforming or improving a little of what we
were and what we had before. He is such a master that
when He takes us in His hand He is going to make us
wholly new. It is His task to transform the apprentice
into an image of His own Self. It thus is not an improve-
ment of the old, it is entirely a fresh creation. And for
this it demands an utter abandonment. Hence we must
leave all and follow Him. Such is the secret of success.

But as someone has rightly noted, this leaving and
forsaking is more an issue of heart attitude. It is quite

true that the physical side to forsaking is important. In the case of Simon Peter he literally left everything and followed the Lord. His boat, his nets, his family were all laid on the altar: the Lord might do anything He pleased with him. Days would come when Peter had to leave his boat, his fishing, and his family behind in order to follow Jesus. He did indeed forsake everything physically.

Yet even in Peter's case, his abandonment was preeminently an attitude of the heart or will. Yes, physically, he did leave all and followed the Lord; nevertheless, he still had his family, and most likely he even still owned his boat and nets. The abandonment, if real, *must first and foremost be in the heart.* Naturally such abandonment does involve giving expression to it in some physical, tangible fashion. Else the heart can never really be set free from entanglement. The Gospel story of the rich young ruler can serve as a good illustration here (Mark 10.17–22).

ONE DAY a rich young ruler came to the Lord Jesus. He literally ran and knelt down before Him in the midst of the multitude. That was not something easy to do, for if you hold a position or have some possessions, would you ever bring yourself to do what this young man did? Among the crowds he runs and kneels down before Jesus and asks that searching question, "Good Teacher, what shall I do that I may inherit eternal life?" He called our Lord Jesus Teacher and asked Him, What shall I do?—I want to be a disciple, I want to learn of

You; so just tell me and I will do it. The earnestness of this young man! And Jesus said, "Why do you call me Good Teacher? There is no one good but God. If you want eternal life, if you want to be perfect, keep the commandments." The young man replied: What commandments? To which the Lord responded, Honor your father and mother, and so on and so forth. And the young man said, From my childhood I have kept these commandments. Was he honest? He was quite honest. Was he sincere? He was. The Gospel writer says that Jesus looked at him and loved him. And what a look that was: the Lord gazed at him and into him—into his very heart. Christ will not be deceived by appearance; He could never be deceived by words or by expressions. So that His eyes pierced into the heart of this young man, and then He spoke: If you really want to be perfect, sell all you have, give to the poor, and then come and follow Me.

Why was the Lord so hard on this young man? Did not this young man have a desire to follow Him? Did he not express a desire to be a disciple? Our Lord should be overjoyed to have such a man to follow him; a *rich* man, a *young* man, a man of *position*. It should be the privilege and honor of the Lord to have such a disciple, because Jesus was only a carpenter and "unlearned". And yet the Lord put before him such a hard condition: Go, sell all you have, give to the poor, then come and follow Me. Why? Surely not because Jesus wanted his money: the Lord said for him to give to the poor; He certainly did not want it. No, the reason the Lord said Go and sell all you have and give to the poor, was for the purpose of liberating him, releasing this young man's heart from that which held him. By contrast, though, the Lord never had to utter such a hard word to Simon. He merely called out, Follow Me, and Simon Peter left all things behind. And why? Because his *heart* was free from any entanglement with them, and Jesus knew the condition of Peter's heart. But to the rich young ruler the Master had to speak differently and more drastically, because He knew that in *his* heart this young man loved money more than anything else.

THIS MATTER OF FORSAKING is not because the Lord wants something out of you—He himself has *everything*, He has far more to give to you than you can ever give to Him. The Lord says to you to forsake because He knows that this or that thing ties you down, binds your heart, makes you its bondman and slave. In a word, because of it you are not free. And because you are not free, He is not free to do anything with you. Forsaking is to set you at liberty. And once you are liberated, Christ then says, Come and follow Me.

Is there anything which binds your heart today? Is there anything which holds you as a slave? If there is, the Lord's word is: forsake it, leave it, do something with it, be willing to let it go; and then you come and follow Me. But the rich young man turned away sadly. He wanted to be a disciple but he could not, for his heart was caught in the grip of his love for money. He would rather have his riches than have eternal life. You may say, How foolish. But, are we any wiser?

FOLLOWING THIS, the Lord next said (v.23ff.) that it was most difficult for a rich man to enter the kingdom of God. And this word surprised the eleven other disciples. Their thinking was that the more you have the easier you enter the kingdom of God, and that the less you have the harder to enter the kingdom. But Jesus had said that it is hard for the rich to enter the kingdom of God. And thus the other disciples asked, Who then can enter? If the rich cannot—if those who have cannot— then we who are poor and who have not, we have no chance. To which the Lord responded with these words: With man it is impossible, but with God all things are possible.

Such was the reaction of the Eleven. Let us now listen to Peter (v.28; cf. Matt. 19.27). Said he, Lord, we have left all and followed You; what then shall we get? Just here, let us pause and consider for a moment. It is a fact that Peter had forsaken all things and followed the Lord. His heart, as we have seen, was *free* from all things. Yet notice how *impure* was his heart, how mixed was his motive. True, he had left all behind, but he expected some sort of recompense. There was a hint of the mercenary in him. In other words, he had a spirit of bargaining. He was not at all like the rich young man: the latter had counted the cost and concluded that his million dollars was more than what Jesus could offer; he would therefore rather keep his million than follow the Lord. But Peter was more clever. He counted and mused within himself and said, "What do I have—a boat, some nets? Oh, in my entire lifetime of fishing I cannot accumulate a million dollars. But the Lord, He is the Lord of all. If He ever wants fish, fish come; if He wants bread, bread appears. Surely that's good, quite good. I will leave all, Lord, and follow You. But now, what will I get?" What a spirit!

VERY OFTEN when the Lord calls us to follow Him we begin to count our costs. And even after we have given up something for the Lord there is such a spirit of martyrdom in us: How we have given up this and that for Him. What a hero we are! What a sacrifice we have made for the Lord! And because we are willing to do this for Christ we find ourselves waiting and ultimately saying something like this: Lord, now what? Do You mean You take away what I have given up and simply forget about it? Aren't You going to give back something more? Let me say that if our forsaking is in this spirit it is not much to count.

Admittedly the Lord does say, "If you forsake all things and follow Me, I will recompense you in this age a hundredfold—with persecution, though—and in the coming age eternal life. I will." As someone has said, the Lord will never be a debtor to anyone; it is the free grace of God. Yet note that Jesus continued with a parable (cf. Matt. 19.30–20.16) which ended with these words: the last shall be first and the first shall be last. The principle we should remember here is simply this: that in this act of forsaking, do not think because you have renounced something for the Lord you have therefore given great honor to Him or you have added something to the Lord, and that because you have made such a sacrifice, therefore He is bound to repay you in some way. Oh, never enter into this with such a spirit. If you do you will be the last.

With the Lord there can be no bargaining. With the Lord there is no sense of sacrifice. With Him it is a matter of pure love. Why do we leave all and follow Him? Not because He demands but because He loves. Love, not reward, ought to be the heart attitude in this action of abandonment. How well-pleasing it would have been to Jesus had Peter's forsaking of all things been due purely to his love for the Master and not to any expectation of recompense. Forsaking all without expecting anything in return should be the norm of abandonment.

Is it not frequently true in your experience as a disciple, when the Lord points his finger at a certain matter and says this must go if you want to be a disciple of His, that you struggle and count, and feel it is too much of a sacrifice? Why so? Because your eyes are upon this matter or that thing. The more you look at it the more this thing becomes bigger and bigger, until it fills the world. It becomes harder and harder to give up. But when the Lord deals with you and somehow appears to you—when somehow you receive a revelation of himself —that thing goes. And when that thing goes, you do not even have the sense of sacrifice. You instead bow before Christ and say: "Lord, is this a sacrifice? I have nothing to sacrifice. Before Your love there is nothing which can be called by that name. If so, it will rather be a disgrace to You. You who give everything to me (and everything is Yours!), You simply want me to give up something for my good so as to set me free that You may be free to do more in my life; how then can I call this a sacrifice?"

If we truly know the Lord, there *is* no sacrifice. It is only when our eyes are upon the things we are going to forsake that such a sense becomes so great. But if our eyes are upon Christ and if He should attract us and reveal himself to us, then there is no sacrifice. And because there is no sacrifice, there is no bargaining. We do not expect the Lord to return in kind or in quantity. The Lord *will*, but that is up to Him. Let us not expect it. Let us see, rather, that it is a matter of love.

Let us not harbor a kind of complex whereby we say: "Oh, the Lord is such a hard master; He demands so much. I have to give up this and give up that. What a sacrifice! Yes, He will return to me a hundredfold, but He has said it will be with persecution! Yes, He will give me in the coming age eternal life, but what about this present age? Death?!?" What a mentality we can get ourselves into. Do not develop a complex such as this. Rejoice if He says forsake. It is a great privilege. The Lord honors us by calling us to forsake because He wants us; He does not cast us aside. He is willing to accept us as His disciples!

✳

BUT A SECOND CONDITION involved in discipleship is

*committal.* If you are not committed fully to a master he cannot transform you. As a modern-day student, I choose my professor. If I do not like him, then next term I move on to another professor. But as a disciple of the Lord Jesus you cannot do that. Either you go all the way with Him as your Master or you drop out; and that is the end.

How often we think we are abandoned to Christ, but we are abandoned to Him only insofar as it suits us. When His will and way begin to conflict with our will and way we are ready to part and to depart. That is not committal. Full committal is another and very important condition of discipleship. We have to entrust ourselves to the Lord for better and for worse, for life and for death.

LOOK AT PETER. One day the Lord Jesus was speaking to many of His disciples (see John 6, especially v.60ff.). And He was saying some hard and difficult words to them. So hard that some of those listening left Him. And turning to the Twelve, the Lord asked if they too would go away. And here Peter shone. He answered Him: "Lord, we have known You and have thus fully entrusted ourselves to You. Others may go, but we have no place to go to and no one else to go to. We are stuck with You, for better or for worse. We have burned our bridges behind us, and we have no choice but to go on with You. Yet we are not propelled along this path by some pathetic idea, but by a brilliant idea: You it is who have the words of eternal life. They are hard words to the flesh, we admit, and are not easily understood; nay, they are impossible to act upon by our flesh. Yet they are the words of eternal life, and it is these that we need and must bank on. Hence we are committed to You and to Your words. Your interest is our interest. And we shall cling to You." What a declaration of full committal!

Yet is it something of which Peter or any other disciple can ever boast? Not at all. For immediately following Peter's dramatic statement of commitment to the Lord, we read that Jesus answered him by saying, "Did not I choose you the twelve?" (v.70) It is Jesus Christ who chooses Peter and the rest, and it is He who brings them to such commitment. Blessed be His Name!

How sad, though, that so few know anything of such commitment. There are many disciples today who, when the Lord does not suit them, can just leave off and go. It seems as if they have so many ways to follow and so many places to which to go. But how about *you?* asks our Lord. Yes, sometimes you will be faced with problems, you will be faced with hard words—words which you do not really understand, just as Peter had not understood on that day what the Lord had said. Despite this, however, Peter was fully committed.

You know, our mind is so materialistically oriented; we are so often thinking in terms of clothing, shelter or food. Just like the five thousand to whom our Lord had fed bread and whom He attempted to direct towards the Bread of Heaven—to eat and drink of Him. This would be spirit and life to them and to the disciples. But as the

Lord tried to lead them more towards the spiritual and
moral aspects of salvation and life, He met growing op-
position from the materialistic nature of fallen man.
Many disciples would not take it in, because they considered these words too difficult.

But are we any different? When the Lord attempts
to lead us away from the materialistic and the earthly
into the spiritual and the heavenly, we sometimes cannot
grasp it because we are too occupied with the earth;
things which are tangible are what we think are the real.
So that when the Lord tries to draw us away from the
tangible to the intangible, from the transient to the permanent, we cannot apprehend it. Moreover, many
things happen in our life which we cannot comprehend
at the moment they occur. Are we offended? Are we
hurt? If we have not fully turned ourselves over to
Christ we *will* be offended, and consequently we will go
away. But if we are those who are fully confiding in the
Lord, then on the one hand we *are* offended but on the
other hand we are *not*: We may not understand, nevertheless we hold fast to the course before us. We are stuck
with the Lord and His ways. Not like many of Jesus'
disciples who left off following Him that day. Outwardly they had followed the Lord, but inwardly they had
not. They had not entrusted themselves to Him but had
instead committed themselves to their own selfishness.
They would follow if everything went *their* way and as
long as they could get something for themselves. But
they were quite ready to part ways with Jesus if the
going got too rough.

Many times in our spiritual experience we feel that

probably this will be the parting hour, it is just too hard. The Lord's way is too strange, we do not understand it, we cannot go on. Yet as we look around there is just no way out. And so we are held fast. And if it means "death" for us, we "die" because there is no other way. We simply *have* to go on with Him, come what may. Now this is committal. And such a position was true in the case of Peter. He stuck it out with the Lord. Others may leave but he cannot because there is no other person to whom he can go. This too is a condition of discipleship: that there be full committal to the Lord.

✳

NATURALLY SUCH COMMITTAL cannot but be severely tested. The enemy of our Lord and of all believers will be all out to try to frustrate or break down such absolute adherence to Christ. He will try his best to stir up his old ally, the flesh, so as to cause the collapse of this committal. Peter was himself severely tested, and was found wanting.

You will recall that towards the end of Jesus' earthly life Peter, in depending upon his own flesh, failed completely in this regard. Our Lord in effect was saying that Peter's commitment to Him would utterly collapse when, in foretelling Peter's denial, He said that all of them would be stumbled and offended at Him and become like scattered sheep the moment the Shepherd would be smitten. Yet despite his declaration of loyalty and commitment ("Although all shall be offended, yet

will not I") and despite his words spoken "exceeding ve-
hemently" that even if he must die with Jesus he would
not deny Him (Mark 14.27–31), Peter lapsed back into
his flesh and denied the Lord three times. So that the response of this disciple to his Master's distant gaze—re-
minding him of the Lord's prediction—was to go from
His presence and weep bitterly.

Peter fully realized how he had failed the Master in
his commitment. He recognized the frailty of his flesh
and how utterly undependable it was. But although he
in this moment had been seized by the enemy, the Lord
had prayed for him that his faith might not fail (cf.
Luke 22.31–34). And how wonderfully this disciple was
later restored in that touching scene recorded in John
21. Henceforth this committal was final and permanent.
There was no more wavering, because now Peter trusted
not in his flesh but in the knowledge that his Lord and
Master had of him: "Thou *knowest* that I love thee"
(v.15ff.).

A VERY PATHETIC THING to see today in Christianity is
how believers can quite easily, even more so than Peter,
be offended and can so quickly leave the Lord. It only
shows one thing, that they are not fully abandoned to
Christ; they are only committed to a certain extent; and
if the Lord should go beyond that, they say, No, no—
that's all I am committed. Yet let us remember this, that
if we are not committed to the Lord, He is not committed to us. He can only be fully pledged to those who are

fully pledged to Him. If we are uncommitted, the Master will not hold us to himself. He is willing to let us go our own way. The Lord is not after an unruly crowd, He is after a disciplined army. Let me ask you, What have you entrusted to the Lord? How much can you commit to Him? And how much can He commit to you?

✳

THIS IS COMMITTAL, but we are only in the beginning stage of discipleship. *With the forsaking negatively and the committing positively, only then can the process of transformation begin.* In other words, the school of discipleship really begins right here. Now the class is open. Today you can begin to be under the discipline and the training of the Lord, to begin to let Him transform you to be His disciple. Even very much as Simon Peter made his beginning. And for three years thereafter the Master is found correcting, chastising, training, instructing, teaching, molding, fashioning, and transforming this man Simon. For three whole years, never a day passed without the Lord working in this disciple. And even after three years the Holy Spirit continued the disciplining and the training of this follower of the Master.

As you read the four Gospels you begin to discern the fact that Peter was the one the Lord dealt with more often and more severely than all the rest of the disciples. It so happened that he was such an honest man. Peter was so frank and so open; clearly, he wore his heart on his sleeve. And because of his outgoing and extrovertish nature, he was very much disciplined by the Lord.

✻

SOMETIMES AS I READ the various Gospel accounts I feel
like saying, "Now Simon, why don't you be a little more
clever! Be a little more cautious and less outspoken.
Then you'll less likely be subject to scoldings! Look,
Peter, at the other disciples. When they do not agree or
they have opinions or when they have something to say,
they do not express these to the Lord but they murmur
among themselves. Yet you, Simon Peter, you are a fool,
for you always blurt it out; and this you do *before the
Lord!* And so He is given the opportunity to say things
to you such as, Get thee behind Me, Satan! Oh Peter,
don't you yearn to be more clever as the others are?"

We, like the other disciples, think it safer if we hide
ourselves more, if we learn to be more secretive and less
open and frank. Frequently we have something going on
here but we utter not a word. Or else, if we must say a
word about it we tell it to some friends of ours but never
to the Lord. By doing this we know what we say. And
by so doing we will not get into trouble. But it seems as
though Peter got into trouble with his Master constantly. He was at odds with the Lord and the Lord was at
odds with him all the time. Peter, it appears, was the
problem disciple. The other disciples were no problem,
but he was "the black sheep" in "the family" of the
Lord.

Yet let me ask you to please note this: Had Peter
been cleverer than others and tried to hide things from
the Lord, would he have been able to be transformed in
this way? No, he would have deprived himself of many

opportunities of learning his lessons. Let us see that the Lord delights in honesty in the inward man. The Lord cannot take delight in some of us because He will not deal with a crooked or evasive heart. If a person wishes to hide something from the Lord the latter will say, All right, hide it; I see it, but go ahead and hide it. He can do nothing more for that person or in that one. If, however, a person is honest and open before the Lord, He can work in that person's life.* If a person really desires the Master to teach him, he must be transparent before Him, not hiding from Him anything but telling Him everything. Let us not be too free before men but let us all be willing and ready to be exposed before the Lord, corrected, and, if need be, to be scolded. You know, the one who learns more and faster is the one who is corrected more. Am I not right? Hence do not be too clever. I have discovered that there are too many clever men and women today, even among believers. They are humanly clever but divinely foolish.

Now because Peter was so open and frank with the Lord, he was very much dealt with by Him. Yet thank God that Christ dealt with him so; for it was His grace. If with us the Master should say, "I leave you alone," you and I are finished. But if He is willing to bother

---

* Just here it should be made clear that I am not subscribing to the thought that Peter's personality being such, he cannot help but be this way; and that because he is such he is therefore good. Not at all. God has made us all with different temperaments, and because the Creator has made a variety of temperaments, there can be no sense of good and evil or right and wrong attached to the different kinds of personality He has created.

himself with us and our problems, as He did with Simon Peter, then let us praise the Lord and thank Him for His grace. Many Christians are so good at covering things about themselves before the Lord that He has to leave them alone by saying, "Well now, if you are so good in yourself, continue that way." And thus He lets them be good with themselves as they are. But if He can witness the fact that we are transparent before Him He will reveal and expose much that is in us.

WE COME FINALLY to the third condition of discipleship —that of *self-denial and cross-bearing.* Let me say that to forsake all or to profess total committal is not a difficult task, relatively speaking. You may forsake all, you may even say "I commit everything to the Lord," yet I believe you will come to agree with me that what is hardest to do is to have what is inside you exposed and dealt with. If this self-life is not being denied, then neither the forsaking of outward things nor the committing fully to the Lord will be of any permanent spiritual value. For sooner or later these outward things will return; and the committal, such as it is, will probably get you into trouble.

Let us see that our forsaking all and our complete dependence upon the Lord are but the indications of our willingness and seriousness in answering the call. The most practical and daily process of true discipleship is in the cross-bearing. This is where the real training lies. That which is within our old man, the natural self, must be revealed and exposed continuously in the light of Christ. God's will and way will bring out the hidden will and way of our own. And these two will clash and wrestle with each other. They intersect each other's path, and in so doing they form the cross we are commanded to bear.

IN THIS MATTER of the training of disciples, please clearly recognize that such a process is not simply to try to induct you into some skill, some knowledge, or some means and ways of doing things. No, no, no. These are the least aspects of discipleship. The training of a disciple is not primarily an outward concern but is preeminently an inward affair. The most difficult thing to train in another person is not his hand. My own hands are very dull, for I have never been trained in their use. In China we boys in the family did not do any work and hence today we do not know how to use our hands in manual work very much. In this regard I sometimes feel ashamed of myself. Nevertheless, even if my hands are dull I can still be trained in their use. But if I have a self-will of my own, my master cannot teach me in the use of my hands. If he who is to train my hands says to me, "Please hold them that way," but I reply with, "Why? I think holding them this way is better," what will be the result? No matter who your master is, he cannot train you. In the face of that self-will, that self-confidence, and that self-centeredness in you, it will be impossible for any master to instruct you in the use of your hands and he will be forced to say, "All right, go your own way." No, it is not a matter of the hands—something outward—it is a matter of the soul—the self-life resident within.

That in essence is *the* problem of discipleship. The greatest hindrance to following the Lord lies in ourselves. If only Christ can be granted the permission to deal with our self-life, then He can do anything and everything with us—which is exactly what we will eventually find in the story of Simon Peter. The Master, now given the right to do so in this disciple's life, is going to deal with his soul until that self-life of his shall recede and ultimately depart and Christ shall increasingly reign in him. And when that thing happens in this man's life it is a transformation. With each instance of dealing it is a coming nearer and closer of Simon Peter to the heart and spirit of the Master. And this is true discipleship.

LET US NOW take a closer look at the life of Simon Peter by means of a few incidents which occurred subsequent to the miraculous catch of fish. Here is the first one we wish to consider, found recorded in Matthew 16.21ff. A situation arises wherein Christ declares that He must go to Jerusalem and there must die. Simon Peter immediately blurts out with: "No, Lord. There must be another way. You do not need to be so foolish. You can attain the crown and the throne without the cross. Be kind to yourself." This disciple has his own mentality, which is a product of his own mind. Peter here is a *self-minded* person. Although it seems, at first glance, that he spoke with good intentions, upon further scrutiny it becomes clear that hidden at the back was his own self-consideration. His mind was not on the things of the Lord but on the things of his own, for this fact comes out plainly in the end: he denied the Lord because basically he was being kind to himself. Peter thought more in line with his own life than the life of God. And he even dared to impose and force his own selfish mind upon his Lord. He was bent on transforming his Master rather than conforming himself to the Master. What a contradiction to discipleship! No wonder, then, that the Lord dealt so harshly and drastically with Peter, because this is something which must be eliminated immediately. Jesus declared to him: "Get behind Me, Satan! You are a stumbling block to Me, Peter; for you do not mind the things of God but the things of men." It is Satan who is in his mind; for Satan is always the force behind self.

ANOTHER SITUATION arose (see Matthew 17.1–7). The Lord took the three disciples up into the Mount of Transfiguration, where Peter looked up and saw Moses and Elijah appearing with Jesus there; and to him it was so good. He was enjoying the company of Moses and Elijah as much as that of the Lord's that he did not wish to see the two depart when they showed signs of leaving (cf. Luke 9.33). Thought he: This is too good to let fade away. But he did not know what to say; yet he had to do or say something quickly, else they would leave altogether. So he blurted out with some words again, but this time how much cleverer he was! Said Peter: Let us make three tabernacles, Lord; one for You of course, but also one for Moses and one for Elijah. By which he meant that then he could enjoy it totally and forever. It was a case of *self-enjoyment*. He enjoyed this great scene so much that he wanted to hold on to it. And for what? For himself; and yet he forgot that there were people in the valley and in the plain who needed the Lord. Here was selfishness manifesting itself once again.

But immediately his opinion was cut across by that of the Father's. God reprimanded the disciple for this by instantly taking away Moses and Elijah. Frankly, I believe they made a much hastier exit because of what Peter said. And then the Heavenly Voice answered Peter, "This is My beloved Son, in whom I am well pleased. You hear Him!" As a disciple Peter was supposed to hear, not to speak. He should accept whatever was provided and be willing to part with whatever was taken away. Yet his sense of self-enjoyment was too great to allow himself to be silent.

STILL ANOTHER INSTANCE comes to mind (see Matthew 17.24–27). And here Peter assumed the place of the Master. He liked to be the head, for that was in his nature—a natural leader who made quick independent decisions. This time some men from the temple who collected the temple tax came to Peter one day and asked,

Doesn't your Master pay the required tax of a half-shekel? Yes, of course, Peter replied. Thus did he involve the Lord in the religious payment of tribute money to the temple. Why did Peter say that? No doubt he had his own reasoning, which probably ran something like this: "The Lord most certainly visits the temple; and He is a good religious Jew; and as a good Jew He naturally would want to pay the temple tribute. Of course the Lord would do that, so I don't even need to ask Him. I know His thought on the matter already." With such reasoning as this, Simon quite naturally would say yes to these men; whereupon Peter went in to ask the Lord for the money. Yet he was not aware that the Lord did not have the money. How this disciple would embarrass Him so. (Yet how often we ourselves do that.)

Nonetheless Peter went in to speak to his Master, but before he could say anything the Lord first asked him this: Peter, from whom will the king collect toll or tribute: from his sons or from strangers? And Peter said: Of course, strangers. To which the Lord replied: Well then, the son does not need to pay.

Do let us see that where the Lord is concerned, we are to take nothing for granted. Our natural reasoning has no place, for He will often surprise us: as the Son, the Lord needed not to pay. Nevertheless, in order to save Peter from embarrassment and so as not to offend the collectors, the Lord said to him: I do not have the money, but I want you to go and fish for it. Do this, and when the first fish comes up, open its mouth; and in it you will find a shekel for you and for Me. Give that to the authorities. And he went and did so.

What an appropriate treatment to prescribe for a quick temperament! Peter might very well wonder when the first fish would bite! And as he was fishing, how he greatly hoped that that fish would come up fast. Yet I think that probably on that day the fish came up very slowly. And as a consequence I believe Peter, while waiting for his fish, learned a great lesson concerning the making of *self-decisions*—to make none independently for the Master nor for himself.

A GREAT MANY other instances could be mentioned. On one occasion (recorded in Matthew 18.21f.) Peter came to Jesus and asked, "Lord, if my brother should sin against me and I forgive him seven times, is that enough?" I do not think it is an easy matter for Peter to forgive like that. It may be easy for others but not so for him. Probably the brother he has in mind here is Andrew. Yet I doubt very much it is Andrew who is the one who offends Peter. More likely in his relationship with his brother, Peter is offended by himself! For Andrew is such a good brother—quiet, unassuming, yet noting every little detail and ever probing, and who has such love for his brother Simon.

Peter, on the other hand, was so quick-tempered. Could it be that Simon was actually the one who sinned against his brother? For most probably Peter became offended not because something was wrong with his brother Andrew but in fact because something was wrong with Peter himself. He might well have misunderstood

Andrew and thus unconsciously thought his brother had offended him—"and so I forgive you." How *self-right-eous* Peter was. Yet are we not often guilty of this very thing ourselves? And hence he believed that if he forgave his brother seven times that that should be sufficient; and he accordingly felt himself so righteous before God. Yet we know what Jesus said in this instance: Not seven times but seventy-seven times!

Self-mindedness, self-enjoyment, self-decision, and self-righteousness. These are some of the self-centered traits which Peter so easily and so spontaneously exhibited in his conduct before the Lord. During these years of association we can see one thing most plainly, which is, that the Master was dealing with this man in the aspect of the self-life. Occasion upon occasion, situation after situation arose to give opportunity for the Master to expose the self which was in this disciple of His. And after each point was exposed it was corrected by the Lord.

BUT WE COME to one last trait of self to be found in Simon Peter—which was that of *self-confidence*. His pride and boasting, which in the instance to follow collapsed completely, were fully dealt with. "If everyone else should be offended," said this disciple to his Master, "I will not. I'm willing, if need be, to die for you!" (Matt. 26.33–35) So confident was Peter in himself here. Yet the result was that he fell to the bottom. He could not even watch with his Master in the Garden of Gethsemane! Where was his self-confidence there? His flesh could not even endure an hour's test. And ultimately we shall find that Peter denied his Lord repeatedly (see Matthew 26.69–75). In other words, this man's pride and boasting fell so completely that he came to the very end of himself.

Notice what the Lord did to deal with him. Jesus simply turned around and *looked* at Peter (cf. Luke 22.61). It is interesting to observe that this is the same word which was used in John chapter 1 to describe how, when Simon first came to Jesus, the Lord had looked carefully at him. And now the Lord turned back and looked carefully at him once again. No word was uttered. It was not necessary. Jesus merely gazed at him and Peter went out weeping. And thus was he brought to the end of himself. In that penetrating gaze of the Lord he saw at last what was in him. He finally perceived what was the whole trouble; he saw in a flash the entire reason why he could not be a good disciple. It was self, just himself, that was the problem. So that he now greatly abhorred himself and went out and wept bitterly. But this shattering experience constituted the beginning of a new life for Peter. Having gone to the bottom, from that day onward he would be going up.

THIS BRIEF SURVEY of Simon Peter's three years with the Lord has not been a very pretty picture. It seems to us that he was so full of faults. His self was so prominent and so strong: strong in mind, in affections, and in will. His opinions were countless, and he was highly self-righteous and self-confident. No wonder, then, that the Master had to deal most persistently with him. But is our flesh any less active and any less strong? Every man's flesh is the same: although it may differ in manifestation, it is the same in essence. And the hidden flesh is even more difficult to be dealt with—yet not because the Lord is ignorant, but because we deceive ourselves into being unwilling to be corrected.

And hence, how we too, like Peter, need this second look of the Lord in our lives—that He will look at us and look through all the hidden things in us. As with Peter, there is no need for words; we know this only too well, for the Lord has already spoken to us too. We come finally, as Peter did, to realize that it is just this self which is the trouble. And it is only when we fall to the bottom of our self that we come to abhor our self. Peter did: he just hated it. He desired never to try to do anything himself anymore. And because of this new attitude of heart he is like soft clay—willing, obedient, tender—in the hand of the Master; and the Master can now mold and shape him in whatever way it pleases Him.

In conclusion, then, we need to notice the heart attitude of Peter in all these dealings. One outstanding trait in this disciple was the fact that he could stand and accept the training. He neither doubted his Master nor sunk into despair nor rose up in rebellion. His heart instead was upon the Lord. His forsaking and committing were for real. He stuck with Christ and accepted everything graciously. He was now in His hand for the Lord to mold and shape him. Thus did Peter learn, even if slowly and haltingly. But then, who ever really learns fast? It is so hard for the flesh to go down into death. But gradually and steadily the Lord was transforming Peter. And although at his denial of the Master he sank to the bottom of his life, afterwards he was steadily raised up in resurrection life to become a disciple who had the resemblance of his Master. And such was what the Lord was actually after in this man's life.

*O Lord, how patient, how long-suffering, how loving, and how full of kindness You are to us. Yet how impatient, how arrogant, how independent and proud we are. We wonder that You simply do not shake Your head and say about each of us, It is finished and done for. How we praise and thank You that once You have apprehended us You will never let us go: You have clearly said You will never leave us nor forsake us: And how we praise and thank You for that.*

*Gracious Lord, deal with us even if we do not want to be dealt with. Today we make a covenant with You: we are committed to You, even though at times it may seem we are fainting— that we are turning our back towards You. But Lord, will You not turn Your eyes upon us? Do look at us, melt us, and break us that we may come to abhor ourselves and at last draw near and stick close to You.*

*We are encouraged, Lord, by what You have done with Your servant Peter. And we too want to go on with You. Help us, O Lord. In Your precious Name we pray. Amen.*

# CHAPTER THREE

# THE CONSOLATION OF DISCIPLESHIP

So when they had broken their fast, Jesus saith to Simon Peter, Simon, son of John, lovest thou me more than these? He saith unto him, Yea, Lord; thou knowest that I *am attached to* thee. He saith unto him, Feed my lambs. He saith to him again a second time, Simon, son of John, lovest thou me? He saith unto him, Yea, Lord; thou knowest that I *am attached to* thee. He saith unto him, Tend my sheep. He saith unto him the third time, Simon, son of John, *art thou attached to* me? Peter was grieved because he said unto him the third time, *Art thou attached to* me? And he said unto him, Lord thou knowest all things; thou knowest that I *am attached to* thee. Jesus saith unto him, Feed my sheep. Verily, verily, I say unto thee, When thou wast young, thou girdest thyself, and walkedst whither thou wouldest: but when thou shalt be old, thou shalt stretch forth thy hands, and another shall gird thee, and carry thee whither thou wouldest not. Now this he spake, signifying by what manner of death he should glorify God.

And when he had spoken this, he saith unto him, Follow me. Peter, turning about, seeth the disciple whom Jesus loved following; who also leaned back on his breast at the supper, and said, Lord, who is he that betrayeth thee? Peter therefore seeing him saith to Jesus, Lord, and what shall this man do? Jesus saith unto him, If I will that he tarry till I come, what is that to thee? follow thou me. (John 21.15-22, with Darby variant added in italics)

WE COME finally to the third aspect of our subject, which is the consolation of discipleship—how we may enjoy the Lord and be enlarged and then endowed with power to bear fruit to the Father's glory. Probably the best way to illustrate this aspect in the life of Peter is to continue with what was shared in fellowship the last time, when we left off with Peter's denial of the Lord after those years of walking with Him as His disciple. Before proceeding further, however, I need to say a few words directly concerning this subject of consolation lest we have a distorted view of it as it relates to discipleship.

WE MAY HAVE THOUGHT that during those three long years before Peter's denial he had never received any consolation as a disciple of the Lord Jesus. If so, then we have an erroneous conception of the place of consolation in our walk with the Lord. We must rid ourselves of the misconception that to be a disciple of Christ is all pain and sorrow and suffering and cost and all these negative things. I fear that too often, when people mention this phrase "disciple of Jesus Christ", the immediate reaction in most of us is that it means a long face, a round shoulder, a downcast look, a sad existence. Is that not our impression? If so, then let us be corrected on this issue.

It is quite true that to be a disciple is not an easy experience. Discipleship does not mean a flowery bed of ease wherein all is rosy and all is smooth sailing; it does not at all mean that there are no problems nor difficulties nor conflict nor trial nor testing. Not so. The life of a disciple is precisely what the word signifies: a *disciplined* life. A disciple's path is not one in which a person can do whatever he likes. It means being disciplined, being put under training, sometimes coming under pressure and strain, and encountering many conflicts and numerous strugglings. Let me hasten to say, however, that if discipleship is *only* that, then who should ever want to be a disciple?

We discover, though, that following the Lord has another side, which is the side of consolation. There are consolations in discipleship. Yes, Peter forsook all and followed the Lord; but was not the company of the Lord more than enough compensation for the people, things, and relationships he had forsaken?

During those years he was with Jesus—in which the Lord was his constant Companion, Master, and Friend —Peter could open his heart to Him and He understood. Whenever Peter was in need he turned to the Master, and the Master supplied that need. Concerning these years of constant intimate living with the Master it is almost impossible to describe the blessing, the pleasure and the joy of being a disciple. For he shared the Master's glory as well as the Master's humiliation. Even though at times Peter was reprimanded by his Master, and very severely, nevertheless, at other times, we find how this same Master would take Peter into His confidence: he was with the Lord on those occasions in which only three disciples were allowed to be present when He did something special.

For instance, Peter and the two other disciples were alone with the Lord when He raised up the daughter of Jairus. Then too, Peter was privileged to be with Him during that momentous event on the Mount of Transfiguration. And even in the instance of the awesome personal agony of the Garden of Gethsemane, the Lord took Peter into His confidence by taking him aside there. How outgoing was our Lord toward this Peter, and this despite the fact that He knew him so well. In view of the accurate though disappointing knowledge which our Lord had of him, how could He open himself so to this man? How could the Master take this man into His confidence? How could He ever look to this man for comfort? Yet He did! In spite of what He knew of Peter, the Lord still went out to him, took him in, shared confidences and experiences with him. Not only were they *together* for three years, but in addition our Lord during this time never withdrew himself from Peter. He went out continually to him; and whether the disciple could respond or not it did not change the Master's attitude towards him in the least. That is comfort, that is pleasure.

Moreover, during this period our Lord sent Peter out with the other ones. Jesus gave them authority to heal the sick, to cast out demons, and to preach the gospel to the poor. And, it should be noted, their mission was very successful. Hence it can be said that during these years Peter enjoyed the Lord very much.

And how do we know? Because when Jesus began to tell Peter and the others that He was soon to leave them, how sorrowful they became (John 16.6,22). That tells it, does it not? If you do not enjoy somebody's company, you will say to yourself when that person announces that he is leaving, Thank God!—Finally! But that is not the kind of reaction displayed here by Peter and the other disciples. We see that they were grieved to the very bottom of their hearts. And from this we know how they treasured the company of the Lord. In this we can perceive what Jesus must have meant to them: He meant everything to them: No one counted more in their lives than did the Lord. If He were gone everything was gone, nothing was left. They had forsaken all to win Christ, and Christ today is more than all to them; so that if Christ should leave them, their lives will be empty and barren. Now that is the Lord, that is the preciousness of our Lord.

We can certainly say, then, that Peter enjoyed the Lord during these three years; and if anyone is with the Lord for this length of time, there must be growth; you just cannot be with Him without growing. Yes, there were periods of drawing back as well as periods of advance. Life is like that. But, taken in its totality, Peter was nonetheless making progress. No matter how deep he fell at the end of these years of discipleship (and it cannot be denied that he took a deep plunge), we nevertheless can see how he had grown in the Lord, both in knowledge and in life. These were the formative years in Peter's life, years in which we see both his failures and his advances. In the Chinese there is this proverb: A child grows by falling. If a child never falls he will never grow; the more he falls to the ground the more he grows up. And that is the way it was with this disciple. He grew by falling. And when he fell to the lowest depths he grew the fastest, and that by the grace of God.

LET ME THEREFORE EMPHASIZE what was said earlier, that Peter's experience in this period was not all suffering and sorrow and correction, and that only after he graduated as a disciple did he begin to know enjoyment and to be enlarged. Not true. These two things—discipline and consolation—go together in anyone's experience as a disciple of Christ. As we advance in the school of discipleship we also make advance in the consolations. The latter is the outcome of the former, the results of the learning and training. The more you follow the Lord and the more you are disciplined and trained, the more you will enjoy Him and the more you will be enlarged and become more fruitful. But contrarily, if you follow the Lord at a distance, you will likewise enjoy Him at a distance and will not grow very much. You may have many leaves but there will be little fruit.

Yet if, like Peter, you follow the Lord closely and allow Him to work with His masterful and skillful hand, then even the Hand that breaks you is a Hand that you wish to kiss, for you enjoy it and are being enlarged by it. By this process you, as did the first disciple, will become more like the Master, and out from within yourself will surely be manifested the fruit of the Spirit of the Master. Such is the consolation of discipleship. And this, in the case of Peter, became very very clear especially when he was being raised up and restored by God after his terrible fall. So as a help to our comprehending better what the consolation of discipleship means I would like to focus our attention upon this "afterwards" in Peter's own experience. And for this we need to read John 21.15-22, since the scene we have in these verses sharpens our understanding of what is the basis for experiencing the fruits of discipleship.

AS WE EARLIER SAW, Peter, in his self-confidence, failed utterly. He denied his Master three times; and upon his doing so Jesus turned back at Peter, who had stationed himself way out in the court. I believe that at this critical moment he was probably just beginning to slip away when the Lord, far inside—but not forgetting Peter though He himself was under accusation and judgment —turned and looked carefully at him in the distance. And, with Peter's face still towards the Lord (we must thank God for that), the disciple saw and caught that gaze and went out and wept.

That was the end of Peter. What was left of him now? Nothing. He was finished. He was reduced to zero. He was supposed by all to be one who stayed on top; and during those three years he himself had struggled to remain as the first. But now where was he? At the bottom. He was not even certain whether the Lord would ever forgive him. That was now his fear. He had gone out, and he had repented, but I am afraid there still lurked doubt in his heart. Although he could have left Jerusalem and gone back to Galilee to forget the whole affair, he did not. He instead lingered in Jerusalem. Somehow he could not leave. Strange, is it not? The Lord was crucified, the Lord was buried, and yet Peter could not bring himself to leave. Perhaps, he thought, there was still hope in the boundless mercies of God. And so he remained in Jerusalem.

And probably during this time the only one who stayed with Peter through the crisis, in a sense to comfort him if he could, was John. Yet I do not believe John *could* comfort him; it was something beyond comforting; nevertheless, John stayed with him.

Here is a lesson for us to learn. Often when a brother or sister in the Lord is in trouble you may not have the ability to comfort that person or help that one out of the problem, yet if you can only stay with this brother or sister and stick with this one, that in itself is help. And John did that very thing; he could not comfort this brother but he stayed with him nonetheless; and for three days Peter was enveloped in darkness. He could no longer be sure of himself; he did not know where he stood, where he would go, what would be his future. He simply did not know. In short, he was a lost soul, adrift in the sea of doubt.

✳

ON THE DAY of resurrection, however, a woman came and reported that someone had taken away the body of the Lord (John 20.2). Upon hearing this news Peter—though he was an older man—ran towards the tomb, but John too ran and, being younger, surpassed him. They came to the tomb. John hesitated, but Peter rushed in. Sure enough, the tomb was empty. The linen cloths that had enveloped the Lord were still in their wrapping, and the head piece was neatly rolled up nearby, but the body was not to be found (John 20.4ff.). He went back to his place wondering what all this could mean.

Had the Lord truly been raised from the dead? If He was, thought Peter, then what about me? Will He receive me or will He reject me? How can I face Him? Peter must have been in great agitation. And then a further report came through some other women, who were told by the angel of the Lord to say this: Go and tell My disciples and Peter that I go to Galilee; meet Me there (Mark 16.7). That brief fragment—"and Peter"—gave the disconsolate disciple a lift to his spirit, a ray of hope: the Lord, after all, had not forgotten him; He still remembered, He still wants me. And then later—still on the day of resurrection—Jesus finally appeared to Peter alone (Luke 24.34, cf. 1 Cor. 15.5). The Bible never reveals to us what took place between them—it is too sacred a moment to be recorded. Peter must have wept before the Lord, and somehow he was restored. And again, but somewhat later, the Master appeared once more to his disciples by the Lake of Tiberias. And there the Lord restored His fallen disciple fully before his companions. How touching, how beautiful, how gracious!

BEFORE GOING ON I feel I must at this point say something about Peter and the cross of Christ. When the Lord went to the cross and was crucified on it, in a very real sense Peter went through death with Him and was raised together with Him. Yet not physically, but spiritually. Physically Peter parted company with the Lord at the cross, but morally and spiritually he was united with Christ in death, because He died that we all ourselves might die. And in a very real sense I think this was the experience of this disciple. When the Lord poured out His soul on the cross, Peter also poured out his soul to the ground.

This disciple went through the deep agony of death—for he wept bitterly; he was finished, ended, and done for; how much lower could he fall, since he was at the very bottom with his self-confidence completely destroyed. So far as Peter's own soul was concerned, he was dead. Yet was this not the real spiritual meaning of Calvary? Was not the cross of Christ meant for the pouring out of the life of the soul? Was it not for this that He died for us all on the cross? And because He died, we too have died. Peter had truly come to the end of himself. The old Peter as Simon was now dead. And if there was to be a beginning it would have to be a beginning with Christ. Simon Peter was dead, finished and ended, but now a new beginning arises. There begins the miraculous work of resurrection. And as we previously learned, on the day of Christ's resurrection the Lord sent word to his disciples and mentioned Peter specifically. How this must have touched his anxious heart. And then the Lord appeared to him personally on the same day to assure him of His love. And again, He lifted him up in full view of his companions. The Lord of resurrection was raising His disciple from death.

Hence I feel that as the Lord began to restore His disciple it was a different person rising up. The old Peter was dead, dead with Christ and crucified on the cross. But the Peter that came out of this death is become a new Peter, established on resurrection ground; and resurrection ground is none other than the ground of Christ our Master.

WITH THIS AS A BACKGROUND, THEN, let us look more closely into this scene which we have recorded in John 21. In that early morning dawn the Lord came to the disciples. He provided breakfast for them, and after they had eaten, He began to speak to Peter in the presence of the others. "Simon, son of Jonah, do you love Me more than these? Do you love Me more than the fire? Remember the fire? You were warming yourself in its glow as I was being judged; I was in coldness but you had warmth. Do you love Me more than the fish and the bread here? Do you love Me more than the ship and the net? Do you love Me more than your companions? Do you love Me more than yourself?" And Simon said, "Lord, You know I'm attached to You." And Jesus asked a second time, "Do you love Me?" Peter replied, "Lord, You know I'm attached to You." And He inquired of him still the third time, "Simon, son of Jonah, are you attached to Me?" Simon was now terribly grieved, and so he said, "Lord, You know that I'm attached to You."

It is not my intention to interpret fully this portion of the Scriptures; I only want to help you, if possible, to feel what the Lord is after in His insistent interrogation. I believe you will come to understand that Jesus is attempting to establish a right and solid relationship with Peter. The relationship between this disciple and his Master is henceforth to be founded only on the ground of pure love—so weak in Peter's estimate yet so true in Christ's mind. The relationship between a master and a disciple must be based on love.

Yet such love seldom if ever comes at the outset. Initially, the heart of a disciple towards his master is probably a heart of fear, or a heart of respect, or even a heart of admiration, but it is not a tie of love. The initial connection between the two is one wherein the disciple attempts to squeeze everything possible out of the master. He tries to get all he can from him and so exhaust the master that he will now become master himself. What a selfish purpose. Here, however, the Lord and Master of all is trying to establish with this one disciple,

Peter, a relationship based on a true and solid ground, even the ground of love.

BUT WHAT IS LOVE? Did Peter love the Master before? Yes, he did. But his love was natural; it was a love that came out from himself. Said Peter in self-assurance and self-strength: "I love You, I'm willing to die for You!" But when the moment of truth came, he discovered he loved himself too much to love the Master. He should deny himself, but he ended up denying the wrong person —he denied his Lord. So that in his terrible plunge Simon Peter's natural love had disintegrated. He knew the truth at last about his love for the Master. It was proven beyond doubt. He today knew he loved himself too much to ever love the Master. He finally recognized that in actual fact there was no love in him. And when Jesus said, "Simon, son of Jonah, do you love Me more than these? Do you truly love Me more than the fire?", Simon thought, "How ridiculous! Love the Lord more than fire? What is fire?"

Obviously Simon did not dare to say this audibly since his own recent experience told him and proved to the world that as a matter of fact he loved fire more than he loved the Lord. And hence the only way Simon could answer Him was, "Lord, You know. I myself don't know anymore; for I've lost all confidence in myself. I'm no longer sure of myself as I once was. You know, Lord, that I'm attached to You, but I can no longer use that other word—love. Yes I do have a feeling towards You, I do genuinely want You, but I cannot say that this is love. I can only say that I feel there is something within me which goes out to You, which ties me to You, so that I cannot get away from You. Somehow—somehow I'm attached to You, and I cannot cut myself loose. But this is the only thing I know. And I have to confess that even *that* comes from You, it's not from me. It is You who attracts me; it is You who ties me with the cord of love so that I cannot get away. For it's all on Your basis now, not on mine any longer; it's not what I know, but what You know. You know me far better and far deeper; Your knowledge is real and true; and You know You have apprehended me. You have bound me, I cannot get away; You know all that."

It seems as though Peter has no love at all here, but actually this newfound reticence in him is what the Lord is looking for. This feeling in the disciple is currently very weak, nonetheless it is something very precious to the heart of the Master.

Do not boast and say you have great love for the Lord. The day will come when you shall see there is none in you, that everything must come from Him. Even the little attachment you have to the Lord is drawn by the cord of *His* love. And you cannot get away.

LET IT BE UNDERSTOOD by all of us that the Master does not require you and me to have a great love towards Him, which in reality can only be a manufactured one. You must not do that. Yes, you may be able to create it emotionally, but emotion changes all the time. No, all which the Lord asks of you is this: Do you sense the cord of love which is around your neck? Do you feel you are attached to Him? Do you feel He has apprehended you and that you cannot get away? Then know this, that it is all because of Him. It is He who draws you, it is He who holds you. He it is who knows your true state.

If only today you will have this little amount of love, then the basis of a relationship between the Master and you as His disciple is being laid. Remember that the tie between the Master and the disciple can only be founded upon pure love. And when this pure love is there, what consolation, what communion, what fellowship and enjoyment! You enjoy His presence and He enjoys your presence. You delight in looking at His face and He delights in looking at your face. What enjoyment indeed.

BUT NEXT THE LORD said to Peter, Feed: Feed my lambs —Shepherd my sheep—Feed my sheep. In other words, after a pure love is established between Master and disciple, then surely out of such fellowship and communion there will be enlargement and growth of life. As the apostle Paul has said, If we all, with unveiled face, behold as in a mirror the glory of the Lord, we shall be transformed into the same image from glory to glory even as by the Lord the Spirit (2 Cor. 3.18). As the two of you—Master and disciple—enjoy each other's company, the Master's face will quite naturally begin to become your face. Spiritually a transformation commences to take place within you, and soon you begin to look like Him. More and more you fade and He is increased in you. And as the Master is reproduced in you, surely that which is upon the Master's heart becomes your task, namely, Feed my lambs.

Discipleship as we have said is unto service, unto ministry. Recall how at the very beginning of our study of Peter's life we saw that the Lord had said to him: Come and follow after Me and I will make you a fisher of men. Here, though, the Lord says, Feed my lambs. Peter's service to the Lord was to bear a double meaning: he was not only to cast the nets and bring in many to the kingdom of God but also to take care of the sheep among the flock of God. There is a vast difference, however, between a fisherman and a shepherd. A fisherman can be a very rough, hard, cruel person. Perhaps because I do not fish I often think of a fisherman in cruel terms. I can only see how sharp and crooked is the hook! How rough and cruel on the poor little fish! But a shepherd is quite different. If you deal with a lamb too harshly it will die. From a fisherman to a shepherd—what a change is to be wrought!

THIS LIFE OF PETER is unquestionably being transformed. And subsequently, in the book of Acts and in Peter's own epistles, we find this transformation unfolded before us and completely fulfilled. On the side of service, we see how this disciple caught many fish and how he also shepherded the flock. How effective was Peter in opening the door of the kingdom to the world: On Pentecost three thousand were saved: Later on five thousand were brought in: And through him the gospel to the Gentiles was preached. How fruitful Peter was wherever he went. How he strengthened the church at Jerusalem as well as the dispersed among the Gentiles, as we find in his epistles. And ultimately he was to be one of the foundations of the New Jerusalem.

Note too the transformation in Peter's personal character. The Peter we witness in Acts was but the development or enlargement of the Peter we see at the end of the Gospels. He could now patiently tarry with the other 120 disciples in the upper room for ten days praying and fasting. No longer was he impatient as before, saying "I go a fishing" (John 21.3). He was given such revelation of the word of God that his understanding and appreciation of the Scriptures was most marvelous. His life was so intimate with the Lord because he was full of the Holy Spirit—so much so that he acted as the spokesman and interpreter of Christ. Peter was also courageous in speaking to the Council which both judged him and possessed the power to kill him, just as it had with respect to his Master: "When they beheld the boldness of Peter and John, and had perceived that they were unlearned and ignorant men, they marvelled; and they took knowledge of them, that they had been with Jesus" (Acts 4. 13). He could also on the night before his supposed execution, rest without anxiety between two soldiers who were chained to him. What peace of mind he had!—for he today was trusting the Lord. Then, too, he was set free from tradition as was proven by his going to the house of Cornelius, a Gentile. He was able to stand for the Spirit's leading, and confirm the truth in the church council held at Jerusalem. And though Peter sometimes did fail, yet how humbly, in the instance at Antioch, he could accept to his face that stern correction from Paul— one who was much younger than he. Furthermore, he was able to praise and to recommend Paul in his own letter, freely acknowledging the gift of grace in Paul. To the very end this disciple was faithful. What a life with the Lord and what a fruitful life for the Lord!

YET THERE IS STILL another point worth looking into in this incident before us from John 21. Among other things recorded there, the Lord said these words to Peter: When you were young you went anywhere you wanted to, but when you are old someone will take your hand and lead you to where you will not like to go. And He goes on to signify the death by which Peter will glorify God. The life of a disciple is a martyr's life. By a martyr's life is meant that a person does not live for himself, he lives for someone else—for God. It matters not whether your walk with God ends up in your being killed, massacred, crucified or whatever.* That is not

---

* Tradition says, incidentally, that Peter was crucified by Nero; and when they began to nail him to the cross he is quoted as having said: "I am not worthy to be crucified as was my Lord; place me upside down on the cross."

the point. The point is that a disciple's life is a martyr's life lived out for others. Henceforth Simon Peter did not live for himself, he lived for his Lord. And he became like his Lord. People began to see in him the Master himself. And *that* is discipleship, when other people begin to see the Master in your expression, in your behavior, in your relationship with others. And only when the Master is seen and heard in one's life can it then be said that the disciple has truly learned something.

AND LASTLY, after the Lord had spoken all this to Peter, He said to him, Follow Me. What, again? Haven't I followed You all these years? Can't I be graduated now? Shouldn't I today be a master in my own right?

Yes, in a sense, if you follow the Lord intimately for some years you ought to be a small master to somebody else, but that does not mean that you yourself have nothing further to learn. Never feel you have reached a certain point when you need not follow the Master and can demand of people to follow you. They can follow you only if you follow the Master. The Lord is still calling you. He still continues to beckon: Follow Me. And why? Because our Master is so inexhaustible. In His wisdom, in His power, in His moral glory, in His character, He is truly inexhaustible. Oh the wonder and riches of Christ our Master! It will require eternity to learn all of Him. Hence comes the call again and again, Follow Me. After all these years of intimate relationship with the Lord, the word from the Master still comes to

Peter the disciple: Follow Me. Are you, too, still following Him? A disciple forever is a disciple indeed.

But look at what Peter does at this moment. As he commences to follow the Lord, he sees another one coming too—his good friend John. And the curiosity and character of the old Peter comes clean to the front once again: Lord, what about this man? You told me I would follow You to death, You told me that. Well now, how about him? Will he die too? We can plainly see from this that Peter is not yet perfect. Listen to what the Master said in reply: If I want him to live until I return, what is that to you?

Peter had expected that if the Lord wished *him* to follow Him to death, then everybody else who follows the Lord must also go to death. Otherwise, he thought, it is unfair: How can the Master expect me to die in following Him but let my friend John live until He comes back? That's too much. It's too easy on John. But the Lord said: What is that to you? Come, and follow Me. You just follow Me, and never mind what happens to others.

✻

HERE I WOULD LEAVE YOU with a brief word of warning. If the Lord has touched your heart and you feel constrained to respond to His call and are willing to go all the way with Him, it may be that by His grace He calls you to follow Him to the *very* end—that is, even to death. But be careful. You may be tempted to look around and say, What about my companion? If I follow the Lord and I die but he can get by so easily by not needing to suffer, am I being too foolish?—I'll be a disciple in the same way he is!

Let me say this to you. Please do not look around. Yes, others may, but you cannot. If it is the Lord's will that others may follow Him and pursue a path of ease and comfort but for you it is His will to live a hard and difficult life, that is His business, not yours. Do not be tempted. Such thinking can offer a real hindrance to your ongoing in Christ. No, do not think and consider like that. Instead, hear what the Lord says. The Lord declares: What is that to you? Follow Me.

Hence the last yet continuing word from the Master to any of His followers can only be this re-affirmation of the call to discipleship: Follow Me!

*O dear Lord, how we praise and thank You that You are not a hard Master; You are a loving Master. You are that ocean of love and we would be lost in You there. How we praise and thank You that You have drawn us with Your glory, even Your loving Self. You have put a love in our hearts, and we are tied to You; and we are more than willing to be tied in this way. For O Lord, it is a pleasure to be with You; it is a delight to learn of You. Your yoke is easy, Your burden is light—because You have loved us and have plant-ed that same love in our hearts.*

*How we do praise You that You have not cast us away, but You have taken hold of us in Your pierced hands and are molding and shaping us unto Your glory. We thank You, Lord, that You have led us thus far and we believe You will lead us to the very end. For we know whom we have believed and we are persuaded that You are able to keep that which we have committed to You against that day.*

*We are in Your hands now, Lord. And we pray that You may work out Your purpose in us. We pray we may be holy, we pray we may be transformed by Your Spirit, so that Christ may be seen and heard, so that many may be brought to You, and that Your church may be built and helped. And, O Master, may we not be those who are continually looking about trying to find an easy way out; but may we set our eyes upon You and, never minding the others, always follow You.*

*So Lord, with confidence not in ourselves but in You our Master, we come and commit ourselves fully to You. And we want to praise and thank You beforehand, knowing that You never fail and that You will bring everything to perfection unto Your glory. We pray in Your precious Name. Amen.*